Saving Scruffy

Misha Herenger

Illustrated by Jan Lieffering

Rigby®

A Harcourt Achieve Imprint

www.Rigby.com
1-800-531-5015

Bruno sat at the window
and watched the street below.

All at once, he gave a big
MEOOOOOW!

"What is going on, Bruno?"
asked Yuan from the next room.

Yuan looked past Bruno.
He saw a scruffy brown cat
on the sidewalk.
When the cat saw Yuan, it ran away.

Yuan went outside to find the cat.
Bruno stayed inside and looked mad.

"Here, kitty! Here, Scruffy!"
called Yuan again and again.
But he couldn't find the cat.

"I don't think Scruffy has a home,"
Yuan told his mom.

"He might be lost," said Mom.

"Maybe we should catch him,"
said Yuan.

The next day, Bruno gave another big
MEOOOOOW.

Yuan knew that Scruffy must be back!

Yuan took some cat food outside.
After Scruffy ate, Mom picked him up.

Yuan and Mom took Scruffy
in a taxi across town.
They went to see the vet.

The vet frowned and said,
"This poor cat needs food and
someone to take care of him."

"Mom, can we keep Scruffy?"
asked Yuan.

"That's fine with me, but what will
Bruno say?" asked Mom.

"He'll say MEOOOOOW!"
said Yuan.

And that is just what Bruno said.
He wasn't happy about having
another cat in the family.

But before long, Scruffy and Bruno
were best friends.